Hydrangeas

CAPE COD AND THE ISLANDS

JOAN HARRISON

Schiffer Publishing Ltd

4880 Lower Valley Road, Atglen, Pennsylvania 19310

Designed by Justin Watkinson
Cover by Bruce Waters
Type set in FilosofiaGrand/BauerBodni BT

ISBN: 978-0-7643-4055-0
Printed in China

Schiffer Books are available at special discounts for bulk purchases for sales promotions or premiums. Special editions, including personalized covers, corporate imprints, and excerpts can be created in large quantities for special needs. For more information contact the publisher:

Published by Schiffer Publishing Ltd.
4880 Lower Valley Road
Atglen, PA 19310
Phone: (610) 593-1777
Fax: (610) 593-2002
E-mail: Info@schifferbooks.com

For the largest selection of fine reference books on this and related subjects, please visit our website at **www.schifferbooks.com**
We are always looking for people to write books on new and related subjects. If you have an idea for a book, please contact us at proposals@schifferbooks.com

This book may be purchased from the publisher.
Please try your bookstore first.
You may write for a free catalog.

In Europe, Schiffer books are distributed by
Bushwood Books
6 Marksbury Ave.
Kew Gardens
Surrey TW9 4JF England
Phone: 44 (0) 20 8392 8585; Fax: 44 (0) 20 8392 9876
E-mail: info@bushwoodbooks.co.uk
Website: www.bushwoodbooks.co.uk

to HYDRANGEA *lovers* EVERYWHERE.

CONTENTS

ACKNOWLEDGMENTS

I am deeply grateful to the many Cape & Island residents who generously shared their beautiful gardens with me. You have reinforced my belief that gardeners are some of the most wonderful people in the world. I include in that number fellow members of the Cape Cod Hydrangea Society, who have also become dear friends.

This project began when Eric Linder of Yellow Umbrella Books in Chatham pointed me in the right direction. I will be forever grateful for his encouragement and support.

Special thanks go to the wonderful people who helped make this project a joyful process along the way: Mal and Mary Kay Condon of Nantucket for generous assistance and memorable hospitality;

Joyce Cornwell for escorting me around Martha's Vineyard with gentle kindness and delightful humor; Katie McConnell for above-and-beyond assistance in photographing her beautiful wedding flowers; and Joan Brazeau, traveling companion and friend, for making me laugh when a good laugh was just what was needed.

My family, as always, has been solidly in my corner. Thank you for understanding and supporting the hydrangea mania that seems to have taken over my life. I have recently been blessed with a dear little granddaughter whose arrival has made me positively gleeful at the thought of one day introducing her to my pals, the hydrangeas. Welcome, dear little Charlotte Maisie, to the wonderful world of hydrangeas.

WATER, WATER EVERYWHERE

Hydrangeas love water. The climate of Cape Cod and the Islands is similar to the maritime regions of Japan where most hydrangeas originated, which is why the flowering shrubs thrive here. They feel at home. Plentiful water along with good doses of fog and mist create the ideal climate for these moisture-loving plants.

Crossing the Sagamore Bridge or the Bourne Bridge transports the traveler to a world surrounded by water: Cape Cod Bay to the north; the Atlantic Ocean to the east; Nantucket Sound to the south; and the Cape Cod Canal to the west. Although Cape Cod is technically a peninsula, it feels like an island, larger, certainly, than Nantucket and Martha's Vineyard, but with that same sense of being separated from the mainland by water. Perhaps this is why visitors feel they are entering a world apart, far removed from routine cares.

Cape Cod's land mass is dotted with hundreds of ponds and lakes. Anyone flying over it can easily get an impression of more water than land below. Countless inland marshes, rivers, and creeks add to the volume of water throughout the Cape & Islands while shorelines are dotted with bays, harbors, and inlets large and small. From the salt water of the ocean beaches to the fresh water of kettle ponds, water is everywhere.

Blue hydrangeas and sea grass accent the artists' shanties alongside Hyannis Harbor.

Hydrangeas edging a lawn at Wychmere Harbor Club, Harwich Port.

Blue hydrangeas beside a deck overlooking a section of Bass River.

Sea grass and a mound of blue hydrangeas at the Chatham Bars Inn.

A peaceful Bass River scene.

Mophead and lacecap hydrangeas are often planted near each other, in this case in a yard on the South Yarmouth side of Bass River.

This long lush row of blue hydrangeas is on a property directly across the street from Oyster Pond in Chatham.

A foggy morning in Chatham.

Hyannis Harbor.

On the wharf in Nantucket.

Oyster Pond, Chatham.

Straight Wharf on Nantucket.

Edgartown Harbor.

Edgartown Harbor, Martha's Vineyard.

Waterfront property in West Dennis.

Hydrangeas peeking through a fence to see what the neighbors are up to. The beach in West Dennis is in the background.

Wequassett Resort on Pleasant Bay.

The arch frames a view of Edgartown Harbor on Martha's Vineyard.

Hydrangeas along a path at Wequassett Resort.

Pink hydrangeas line a fence in Edgartown.

This walkway is bordered by blue hydrangeas on one side and the water of Hyannis Harbor on the other side.

'Annabelle' hydrangeas overlooking Sesuit Harbor in East Dennis.

Early morning, Sesuit Harbor, East Dennis.

Edgartown Harbor.

AT HOME WITH HYDRANGEAS

Hydrangeas grace the gardens of homes from the most sophisticated to simplest cottage style all over the Cape & Islands. Their vibrant and voluptuous blooms accent front doors, spill over fences, border driveways, surround decks, and otherwise bring cheerful spots of color wherever they are planted. Whether the look desired is classic and formal or carefree and relaxed, hydrangeas are just right.

With their long bloom time, hydrangeas are an asset to the home garden throughout the growing season. The shrubs are equally effective alone, as specimen plants, or massed together to create rivers of color. Blue hydrangeas are the norm, but pinks, purples, and whites also provide lively accents.

Hydrangeas can be spotted in front yards, side yards, and back yards. They fill pots that are placed near front doors, around sheds, and wherever they can be easily seen from inside the house. New residents see how gorgeous they look in neighbors' yards and rush to the garden centers to get some for their own properties. This contagion of beauty makes clear what natives and newcomers alike seem to know intuitively: hydrangeas are the quintessential flower for the Cape Cod garden.

Both the weather-stained shingles and the lush hydrangeas are classic elements of a Cape Cod home.

Lacecaps in early July are a lovely addition to Cape Cod times.

Hydrangeas accenting the front door of a Cape Cod home.

Clearly the home of a hydrangea lover.
Welcome sign by Hanson artist, Elaine Wright.

A profusion of hydrangeas fill the front yard of this house near Bass River in South Yarmouth.

It won't be long before this hydrangea takes up more space on the crushed shell driveway.

A front yard in Harwich Port filled with hydrangeas and roses.

The lovely white flowers of *Hydrangea arborescens* 'Annabelle' light up this South Yarmouth front yard.

The shape of these hydrangeas puts one in mind of a whale breaching the water.

Roses and hydrangeas are frequent companions in the sea air.

A Cape Cod house in Fourth of July colors.

White Annabelles and pink and blue mopheads grace this Chatham home.

Hydrangeas flourishing at this Chatham cottage near Oyster Pond.

Blue hydrangeas echoing the blue of the Bandtime banner.

The tree with the under planting of hydrangeas provides a focal point in this Nantucket driveway.

Blue mopheads on a stone wall in East Dennis.

A riot of hydrangeas along Route 6A in Yarmouth Port.

Blue lacecaps flowing over a fence in South Yarmouth.

A Harwich Port garage accented with healthy hydrangeas.

The garage door's hardware could represent "C" for Chatham, the setting for these soft blue hydrangeas.

Lacecaps along the fence of one of Edgartown's lovely Greek Revival homes.

Blue hydrangeas and white impatiens create a lovely curve on this Edgartown property.

Hydrangeas provide cheerful color
at the entrance of this Nantucket home.

Blue hydrangeas beside a porch in
Edgartown, Martha's Vineyard.

Deep purple mopheads stand out beautifully against weathered shingles on Nantucket.

White Annabelles light up the woodland side of this Martha's Vineyard property.

One of the Oak Bluffs gingerbread houses accented with blue mopheads.

Lacecaps with white outer sepals against the white trim of this Oak Bluffs gingerbread house in the campground.

A long curving Nantucket driveway lined on both sides with hydrangeas.

A Martha's Vineyard home with hydrangeas across the front of the house and in the side yard beyond the gate.

Hydrangeas used effectively in this Harwich back yard where lacecaps soften the shed and white Annabelles light up the woodland background.

A cottage-style front garden filled with hydrangeas in South Yarmouth.

The birds must be happy to live in this beautiful Yarmouth Port setting.

Clean lines with softening blue hydrangea accents on Oyster Pond in Chatham.

A charming Cape Cod home in South Yarmouth.

HYDRANGEAS FOR SALE

Hydrangeas are in high demand as summer approaches. Regional garden centers are well stocked in the spring and early summer, ready for the hordes of Cape and island residents looking to add one or two hydrangeas to their gardens. It's not uncommon to go with the intent of buying one and coming home with many.

With their gorgeous blooms hydrangeas lend themselves to naturally striking displays at the garden centers where their beauty is both admired and desired; the perfect mix of aesthetics and commerce. Early July is a popular time for hydrangea festivals at the nurseries, a time when these stars of the garden are celebrated with special programs including speakers, art in the garden, and, of course, special sales on hydrangea plants.

Hydrangea fans swap information about where to find interesting collections of cultivars. 'Nikko Blue' is a locally popular offering with a long track record of performing beautifully in this climate and new offerings are developing fans of their own. For a hydrangea lover there is nothing like happening upon an exciting new variety that was previously unknown. Many gardeners rejoice whenever they spot the enticing words: *Hydrangeas for Sale.*

Hydrangeas for sale inside the shade house at Hyannis Country Garden.

Country Garden in Hyannis with garden art in the front including what could be called "Hydrangeas for Sail."

These hydrangeas in Country Garden's shade house look as if they are trying to escape to the outdoors.

Twist-n-Shout

With a botanic name like *Hydrangea macrophylla* 'PIIHM-I' it's no wonder that most prefer to use the common name for this shrub: Twist-n-Shout!

This lacecap is in the Endless Summer Collection so you can be sure it will bloom on both new and old growth.

Lacy pink or blue flowers [...] dark, glossy le[...] Shout will grow b[...] morning sun and [...] compost or co[...]

Prune Twist-n-[...] unsightly gr[...]

Country Garden provides helpful signs to help hydrangea lovers make their selections.

The hydrangeas are ready for customers on the first morning of Country Garden's hydrangea celebration in early July.

Fresh hydrangea blooms for sale at a stand in downtown Nantucket.

Plenty of fresh hydrangeas available for eager customers.

Many of these pink hydrangeas will turn blue in the generally acidic soil of the Cape & Islands.

Here's what usually happens when a hydrangea lover goes off to buy "just one" hydrangea.

Hydrangeas for sale at Hart Farm
Nursery and Garden Center in Dennisport.

Many selections of hydrangeas
are available at Crocker Nurseries.

Blue mopheads at Crocker Nurseries.

Blue 'Penny Mac,' white 'Portuguese White,' and pink
'Invincibelle Spirit' at Crocker Nurseries in Brewster.

Agway of Cape Cod stocks many varieties of hydrangeas
at their two locations in Dennis and Orleans.

Blue mopheads at Green Spot
Garden Center in South Yarmouth.

Many mophead and lacecap varieties are displayed
at the Condon's Nantucket Hydrangea Farm.

The office at the Hydrangea Farm on Nantucket
has views of hydrangeas from every window.

'Mathilda Gutges' at Mal & Mary Kay
Condon's Hydrangea Farm in Nantucket.

Hydrangeas are planted both in containers and in
flower beds all around the property at the Condon's
Hydrangea Farm in Nantucket.

Jardin Mahoney, voted "Best Garden Center/Nursery" by *Martha's Vineyard Magazine* for several years running, supplies hydrangeas for countless Martha's Vineyard customers.

The entrance to Jardin Mahoney on Edgartown Vineyard Haven Road.

Fresh cut hydrangeas for sale at the Flower Pot Nursery & Florist in Centerville.

NANTUCKET BLUE HYDRANGEA SPECIAL

'Nantucket Blue' is one of many hydrangea varieties offered at Jardin Mahoney.

'Nantucket Blue' at Jardin Mahoney.

The lacecap 'Blue Cassel' at Jardin Mahoney.

'Limelight' paniculatas at Jardin Mahoney.

Donaroma's, Martha's Vineyard.

Potted hydrangeas for sale inside
the garden store at Donaroma's.

Healthy plants in a lovely
setting at Donaroma's
Nursery.

A COLORFUL WORLD

Vibrant colors accent the Cape & Islands in the summertime, celebrating the season of sun, sand, and surf. As if in happy agreement, hydrangeas echo the blue of the ocean, the pink of sunsets, and the white of the frothy waves delighting children at the beach. Multicolored flowers are a surprising gift of Mother Nature as if she has decided to take on the persona of a Hollywood producer intent on creating exuberant extravaganzas.

The region is known particularly for blue hydrangeas, with blue shades ranging from pale blue to a deep cornflower blue. A similar range in color can be found if pink flowers are desired, from pale pink to a rich, deep pink. Purples include pale lavender to the kind of deep purple that makes a neighboring gardener say, "I want a cutting of *that* one!"

The varied colors of hydrangeas blend beautifully with other flowers and with each other. Popular color combinations include classic blue and white, cheerful yellow and blue, eye-popping pink and chartreuse, and cooling tones of blue and purple. Local gardeners have an extensive palette with which to create their favorite color combinations. Just add an American flag to a garden with blue hydrangeas and instantly the garden is ready for the Fourth of July.

Three cheers for the
RED, WHITE, & *BLUE*!

A charming pink-and-white gingerbread house in the Oak Bluffs campground, Martha's Vineyard.

The pink and purple hydrangeas add more eye-popping color to the scene.

The hydrangeas look as if they'd happily join a conversation on the porch.

The lacecap 'Fasan' at Hart Farm in Dennisport.

Pink mopheads on the village green in Orleans.

Cityline® 'Paris' at Country Garden in Hyannis.

'Ravel' at Mal Condon's Hydrangea Farm, Nantucket.

Blue and white lacecaps.

It is easier to control the color of hydrangeas in containers than those planted in the ground.

Blue and white: a classic color combination.

'Angel Wings' at the Condon's
Hydrangea Farm, Nantucket.

Pink and purple mopheads alongside
a South Yarmouth garage.

Purple flowers with blue eyes.

Blue and purple mopheads with white Annabelles on Nantucket.

'Purple Majesty' in the front yard of a Yarmouth Port home.

Blue lacecaps and the white arborescens variety 'Incrediball®.'

The lacecap 'Juno' at the Condon's Hydrangea Farm, Nantucket.

The intense color of this hydrangea is known by neighbors as "Jane's Purple."

Lacecaps look right at home with purple coneflowers.

It is interesting to watch unusual coloration develop.

Multicolored blooms are more often spotted in late spring and early summer when the flower color is still developing.

Color variation extends to hydrangea foliage. Pictured here are the lime green of 'Lemon Daddy' and the glossy dark green of 'Alpenglühen.'

A multicolored lacecap spotted on Nantucket in mid-July.

The rich colors of 'Masja' at the Condon's Hydrangea Farm on Nantucket.

Cape Cod Creamery, South Yarmouth.

Blue mopheads with yellow daylilies at Wequassett Resort on Pleasant Bay.

When the hydrangea color develops more fully it will be a strong blue accent against the yellow Oak Bluffs house.

Along a walkway at Wequassett Resort.

A tapestry of color along an Edgartown fence.

Rich late season color
in hydrangeas resting
on a sundial.

FENCES WITH
FLORAL ABUNDANCE

Hydrangeas can be corralled by fences, but not restrained. Their exuberant nature impels them to break the boundaries, as if calling out to passersby, "Look this way! See how gorgeous we are? Aren't you impressed?"

It's as if hydrangeas use fences as props specifically to set off their own beauty. They hug them, drape themselves over them, coyly peek through their rails, and sometimes lean against them affectionately. Sometimes entire sections of fences disappear under a riot of colorful blooms.

White picket fences seem to call for hydrangeas, especially those with blue flowers as there is nothing quite so pleasing as that classic blue and white combination. The style of fence can set either a formal or informal tone, with the hydrangeas adapting easily so that they always look appropriate.

Edgartown residential fence, Martha's Vineyard.

Hydrangea hugging a fence in South Yarmouth.

Blue mopheads hanging over and peeking through an East Dennis fence near Sesuit Harbor.

Blue hydrangeas spilling through a Harwich Port fence.

Blue mopheads crowding a Nantucket fence.

Sometimes a fence sets off the beauty of the hydrangeas behind it.
This fence with its elegant curves is located in Harwich Port near Wychmere Harbor.

The fence may separate the hydrangeas and the roses, but they are no less compatible as a result. The sand dollar stepping stone adds a charming accent.

'Limelight' paniculatas at
Heritage Gardens in Sandwich.

Nantucket hydrangeas enjoying dappled light.

Clearly these Chatham hydrangeas
are happy with their location.

An abundance of the paniculata variety 'Limelight'
at the entrance to Heritage Gardens.

Hydrangeas spilling over a Pleasant Street fence, Nantucket.

These flowers of the paniculata 'Limelight' almost look as if they are resting their chins on the fence.

A classic look: blue hydrangeas on a white fence.

The curved fence contains a cluster of hydrangeas.

This Nantucket fence in full sun is barely containing the hydrangeas.

Blues on a white fence in West Dennis.

White Annabelles with grasses.

These Harwich Port hydrangeas seem
to be heading toward the street.

A curved fence in a Harwich Port garden.

A few blues peeking through this Edgartown fence.

Dark blue hydrangeas really stand out against the white of the fence.

Many escapees from this Nantucket fence.

Hydrangeas are happy in sea breezes in Edgartown, Martha's Vineyard.

A visitor to this Martha's Vineyard home will have to share the seating space with the resident hydrangeas.

Deep raspberry hydrangeas spill over a curved Nantucket fence.

SINGING THE BLUES

More than any other flower, blue hydrangeas complete the classic look of summer gardens on the Cape & Islands. Perhaps because blue flowers are rare in the plant world, the enormous blue flower heads call attention to themselves in an unsubtle, carefree way, much in keeping with the relaxed atmosphere of this region where vacationers come to get away from the cares of the world.

Like the ocean, the list of words used to describe all the shades of blue to be found seems endless: soft blue, French blue, gentian blue, sky blue, rich blue, Persian blue, flax blue, cornflower blue, cobalt blue, powder blue, and so on off to the horizon. A garden could be filled just with the different varieties of hydrangeas with flowers in all the shades of blue, a veritable sea of blue.

Varietal names reflect the importance of blue flowers: 'Blue Billow;' 'Blue Danube'; 'Blue Deckle'; 'Blue Eyes'; 'Blue Prince'; 'Blue Wave'; 'Decatur Blue'; 'Fischer's Silver Blue'; 'Ice Blue'; 'Nikko Blue'; and 'Teller Blue'. No matter what the name, blue hydrangeas can all be described with one umbrella term: *Heavenly Blue*.

A sea of 'Nikko Blue' at a beautifully landscaped Orleans home.

These pale blue lacecaps are at one end of the color spectrum for the blues, which range from very pale blue like this to rich deep blues.

Lavender blue hydrangeas with hints of turquoise.

A graceful spill of mopheads from the side of a porch.

The front office windows of A Beach Breeze Inn in West Harwich allow views of the blue hydrangeas outside.

Blue lacecaps on Nantucket.

Blue mopheads outside the Children's
Center at Wequassett Resort.

Rich blue flowers with hints of purple.

Chase's Ocean Grove on Old Wharf Road in Dennisport.

A seating area at a Yarmouth Port home
featuring 'Nikko Blue' hydrangeas.

Endless Summer® hydrangeas in Yarmouth Port.

Famous blue hydrangeas on Shore Road in Chatham.

Blue mopheads along stone wall on Route 6A
(The Old King's Highway) in East Dennis.

Singing the blues in Chatham.

Blue hydrangeas from this same shrub won "Best in Show" at a Nantucket floral competition.

Blue mopheads on the grounds of the Chatham Wayside Inn.

'Brestenberg' at the Condon's Hydrangea Farm on Nantucket.

Stunning blue lacecaps outside an Edgartown home on Martha's Vineyard.

'Blaumeise' is also called 'Teller Blue.' This one graces a garden in Chatham.

Hydrangeas line the steps leading to a
Hyannis Harbor office.

A beautiful mophead spotted on the side of the road in
Chatham near Oyster Pond.

It would be impossible to choose which of these blue
mopheads has the more lovely color.

The lacy edges add to
the beauty of this soft
blue flower.

The deep blue mopheads are quite attention-getting. The variety name is 'Enziandom' and these were seen at the Condon's Hydrangea Farm on Nantucket.

WEDDINGS & HYDRANGEAS, A PERFECT MATCH

For as long as people can remember, weddings on the Cape and islands have been lavishly decorated with the hydrangeas so widely available here. The sizable blooms are featured in bridal bouquets, table decorations, and as garlands decorating garden arches. The generous size of the flowers, the range of colors available, and a plentiful supply of fresh flowers make them a natural choice for weddings, but it is their beauty that makes them so desired.

Tradition calls for the bride to have "something old, something new, something borrowed, and something blue". The "something blue" could be blue hydrangeas in the bride's bouquet. Blue hydrangeas are particularly popular for beach weddings, often displayed in white containers ranging from formal vases to very casual buckets. No matter how they're displayed, they look lovely. Blue hydrangeas combine beautifully with white roses or white orchids for a classic blue and white look. A more casual effect can be achieved by adding a mix of Canterbury bells and Sweet William from the home garden. Blue hydrangeas also look extremely striking with deep purple mopheads and white lacecaps.

Some brides opt for a pink theme and there are many pink hydrangeas that look wonderful with roses, especially when a two-toned effect is created with soft pink combined with a rich deep pink. White hydrangeas can be found throughout the growing season and are easily combined with other colors selected for the wedding. White flowers against the deep blue of a bridesmaid's dress really makes the white flowers stand out. Autumn weddings sometimes feature white mopheads in a bowl filled with ripe cranberries, especially if that rich cranberry color is also used for bridesmaids' dresses. Cheerful flowers that they are, hydrangeas can only enhance the visible happiness of radiant brides.

Hydrangeas and roses seem made for each other. This bridal bouquet is made up of pink hydrangeas with both soft pink and deep pink roses.
Flowers by Katie McConnell, Wild Bunch Studio, Chatham.

Wychmere Harbor in Harwich Port is the setting for this Cape Cod wedding featuring blue and white hydrangeas. *Flowers by Katie McConnell, Wild Bunch Studio, Chatham.*

A distinctive row of healthy hydrangeas borders the lawn where chairs are in place for wedding guests.

The bride has chosen mainly blue hydrangeas for her wedding: medium blue for the ceremony and deep blue for the reception. *Flowers by Katie McConnell, Wild Bunch Studio, Chatham.*

The scene is set for the guests to take their seats before the arrival of the bride and groom. *Flowers by Katie McConnell, Wild Bunch Studio, Chatham.*

Florists can obtain a wide range of hydrangea colors desired for weddings.
Flowers by Katie McConnell, Wild Bunch Studio, Chatham.

This lovely arrangement features white and green hydrangeas.
Arrangement by Bob Sabatalo, Lily's Flowers & Gifts in South Yarmouth.

Cape Cod hydrangeas fill the metal buckets lining the aisle.
Flowers by Katie McConnell, Wild Bunch Studio, Chatham.

The pink hydrangeas lend themselves to a lovely mounding effect on this table centerpiece. *Flowers by Katie McConnell, Wild Bunch Studio, Chatham.*

White mopheads in a chartreuse container make a simple and elegant wedding accent.

White hydrangeas from the home garden can be used to make stunning wedding arrangements. The flowers of the 'Pink Diamond' paniculata create a lacy and ruffled effect.

A reception centerpiece featuring pink hydrangeas. *Flowers by Katie McConnell, Wild Bunch Studio, Chatham.*

Blue hydrangeas with white roses in a bridal bouquet. The bridemaids wore dresses in a rich shade of royal blue and they carried bouquets of white hydrangeas. *Wedding Flowers by Nichole, The Bourne Florist.*

Hydrangea macrophylla 'Blushing Bride,' part of the Endless Summer® Collection, is a natural choice for weddings.

This arborescens variety called Incrediball®
is known for its exceptionally large white flowers,
a good choice for weddings.

Blue and white hydrangeas anchor this vibrant
wedding arrangement. *Flowers by Bob Sabatalo,
Lily's Flowers & Gifts, South Yarmouth.*

Wedding flowers against a background of hydrangeas
planted on the grounds at Wychmere Harbor. *Flowers
by Katie McConnell, Wild Bunch Studio, Chatham.*

A wedding featuring both white and soft pink
hydrangeas with pink roses and a variety of other
flowers. *Flowers by Katie McConnell, Wild Bunch
Studio, Chatham.*

Double flowers make this mophead hydrangea a
knockout and its name, 'Forever and Ever Together,'
makes it a natural choice for weddings.

Lovely floral arrangements line the aisle prepared for this wedding at Wychmere Harbor. *Flowers by Katie McConnell, Wild Bunch Studio, Chatham.*

The urn is filled with soft colors and lovely textures. *Flowers by Katie McConnell, Wild Bunch Studio, Chatham.*

A wedding centerpiece featuring soft green hydrangeas and pink roses. *Flowers by Katie McConnell, Wild Bunch Studio, Chatham.*

The arrangements in the urns are lush and elegant.
Flowers by Katie McConnell, Wild Bunch Studio, Chatham.

A centerpiece comprised of several smaller arrangements in milk glass containers.
Flowers by Katie McConnell, Wild Bunch Studio, Chatham.

The wedding flowers look especially beautiful when seen close up. *Flowers by Katie McConnell, Wild Bunch Studio, Chatham.*

The pink and white color scheme, beautifully expressed. *Flowers by Katie McConnell, Wild Bunch Studio, Chatham.*

White hydrangeas with pink roses. *Flowers by Katie McConnell, Wild Bunch Studio, Chatham.*

Blue hydrangeas for a silver wedding anniversary.

A very Cape Cod look is achieved with this arrangement of blues in a white ceramic basket. *Arrangement by Joan Brazeau, Yarmouth Port.*

An appropriately titled arrangement created for a home wedding.

HYDRANGEAS
WHEREVER YOU GO

Homeowners are not alone in their tendency to add hydrangeas to their gardens. Many Cape & Island business owners make their properties more attractive by planting hydrangeas. These shrubs are both popular and practical; they provide masses of colorful blooms over a long growing season while requiring little maintenance. It's no wonder they can be found everywhere.

Visitors to the area will see hydrangeas around such local attractions as ice cream parlors, gift shops, and art galleries. All kinds of tourist accommodations from cottages to gracious inns plant them in their gardens for the enjoyment of guests and staff alike. Restaurants, golf courses, and yacht clubs are also likely spots for these beautiful plants.

People who live here year round are accustomed to seeing hydrangeas while running errands to banks, supermarkets, and libraries. Hydrangeas are planted outside churches and post offices. If there is a little town park, it probably sports a nice array of hydrangeas. If you travel around the Cape & Islands at all during the growing season, you are bound to see hydrangeas. And they are bound to look beautiful.

Lacecaps leading to the entrance of an art gallery on Main Street in Chatham.

Many beautiful hydrangeas are planted along the fence of this Harwich location on Route 28.

The hydrangea art work on the sign of this Harwich Port gift shop points to the real hydrangeas below.

An eighteen-hole miniature golf course next to the Weatherdeck restaurant in West Harwich features several beautiful hydrangeas.

Blue and pink mopheads capture attention in front of The Riverway Lobster House restaurant on Route 28 in South Yarmouth.

Tale of the Cod, a shop on Main Street in Chatham, specializes in fine gifts and furniture. Its exterior is delightfully accented with blue mophead hydrangeas.

Hydrangeas are used on many signs throughout the Cape & Islands.

A real estate office in downtown Chatham.

The hydrangeas in front of this Chatham antiques shop can't be missed. The deep blue and purple flowers are spectacular.

Outdoor art shows are a popular Cape Cod summertime attraction. The large white blooms of paniculata hydrangeas in late August at a Harwich Port town park are a wonderful example of Mother Nature's art work.

The exterior of this East Dennis church is made
even lovelier with masses of lacecap hydrangeas.

Vibrant hydrangeas can be spotted all around the beautifully
manicured grounds of Wequassett Resort overlooking Pleasant Bay.

The entrance to the clubhouse of the Eastward Ho! Country Club in Chatham offers a magnificent display of hydrangeas and roses.

The bench is located outside some shops in downtown Nantucket, a perfect spot to relax and enjoy the view of mophead hydrangeas.

The pieces of an outdoor chess set on the grounds of a Hyannis hotel are almost as tall as the blue hydrangeas nearby.

Even a parking lot behind shops in Hyannis Center is graced with beautiful hydrangeas.

Lovely mopheads in the peaceful courtyard of
St. Christopher's church on Main Street in Chatham.

Many plantings of beautiful hydrangeas can be found
in the grounds of Nantucket's Siasconset Union Chapel.

Windswept hydrangeas near the dock
for the ferries in Hyannis Harbor.

Masses of mopheads outside The Beachside motel in Nantucket.

Beautiful hydrangeas at the entrance make it a pleasure to do routine banking.

Bismore Park overlooks Hyannis Harbor. Many lush plantings of blue mophead hydrangeas accent the artists' shanties here.

Blue hydrangeas on the grounds of the Harbor View Hotel & Resort in Edgartown on Martha's Vineyard.

WILD
GOOSE
TAVERN

White Annabelles in front of the Chatham Wayside Inn.

The Net Result, a fish market on Martha's Vineyard.

The Oak Bluffs Inn on Martha's Vineyard
is known for the relaxed charm of its front
porch surrounded by hydrangeas.

A HYDRANGEA
FOR ALL SEASONS

The first hydrangea blossoms to emerge in the spring are the pure white flowers of climbing hydrangeas. These delicate-looking blossoms perfume the air with their fragrance while delighting the eye with their beauty. Their heart-shaped leaves cling tenaciously to trees, pergolas, and trellises, providing lush green background color long after the flowers have faded.

Then the macrophyllas take center stage, first the lacecaps, then the mopheads. Lacecap flower heads are a beautiful composite of tiny fertile flowers in the center around which dance the colorful sterile flowers. Lacecap flowers are in their full glorious prime for several weeks in late spring and early summer before they, too, fade. Fortunately, the mopheads are then ready to take over. During the height of the summer season the big round blooms of mopheads predominate, fading eventually to antique colors in the fall when the paniculatas begin to show their colors.

Like the visiting performers at the Cape Playhouse, each hydrangea has a moment when it takes center stage. Later it will be a supporting player when another star commands attention. Together they are an ensemble cast worthy of long sustained applause.

Climbing hydrangeas billow out over this pergola at New England Gardens in South Harwich.

An outdoor shower in South Dennis is attractively hidden behind climbing hydrangeas.

With the door of the outdoor shower open you can see how the flowers cascade inside the enclosure as well.

A climbing hydrangea has made an impressive climb up this tree at Spohr Gardens in Falmouth. The best time of year to view climbing hydrangeas in this region is the first half of June.

The homeowner says it is not only the beauty of the flowers that she enjoys but also their wonderful fragrance.

Climbing hydrangeas on a tree supporting a hammock in South Yarmouth.
Another climbing hydrangea has been planted at the base of the other supporting tree.

Climbing hydrangea flowers are
delicate looking yet sturdy.

Climbing hydrangeas are in full flower when mopheads
are still in the bud stage. This photo was taken in mid-
June in South Yarmouth.

By the middle of July the mophead flowers are
fully developed and the climbing hydrangea in the
background has become a green backdrop.

By early October the mopheads have changed color
completely, from blue to burgundy. Notice how the
florets turn upside down as they age. Later in October
the foliage of the climbing hydrangea turns yellow. In
morning fog it can be breathtakingly beautiful as it
makes the tree glow like a giant candlestick.

A blue lacecap in early August in Chatham.

The formerly blue lacecap in Chatham has aged to pink by early October. Notice how the outer sepals of the lacecap flowers have turned upside down.

Hydrangea arborescens 'Annabelle.' This extremely popular variety sports flowers that are green when they emerge in spring, white for the many weeks of prime bloom, and revert to green when they age.

An oakleaf hydrangea in July. Later in the season the pure white flowers first age to light pink, then a deeper pink, eventually turning a chocolate brown, while the foliage takes on rich fall colors.

The opulent blooms of paniculata hydrangeas at Chatham Bars Inn in August. These flowers come into their glory when the mopheads are starting to fade to antique colors.

'Limelight,' the paniculata hydrangea planted outside Limelights, a garden and consignment shop in South Dennis.

Hydrangea paniculata 'Limelight' planted along the fence near the entrance to Heritage Gardens in Sandwich. This photo was taken near the end of August.

Sometimes the weight of the huge flowers of paniculatas causes them to bend towards the ground.

At a miniature golf course next to the Weatherdeck restaurant in West Harwich, fall colors are evident on the mophead in the foreground which had blue flowers earlier in the season, and the paniculata in tree form in the background. This photo was taken in early October.

Supports help to keep some of these paniculatas upright. This photo was taken in the parking lot of the Hyannis Yacht Club in mid-September when the flower color was turning from white to pink.

Paniculatas outside the Beach Shop at Chatham Bars Inn.

A well established
paniculata on Bank
Street in Harwich in
early September.

A paniculata trained as a tree in Sandwich. This photo was taken in late August.
The flowers will eventually turn pink then a deep shade of burgundy.

THE INSIDE STORY

Not content to have profusions of hydrangeas in gardens all over Cape Cod and the Islands, residents love to bring the flowers indoors as well. Hydrangeas in the home take many forms, all of them ideally suited to indoor living in this part of the world, where natural beauty is valued and celebrated.

During the height of the season, hydrangeas are popular cut flowers providing attractive color accents in all parts of the house. Part of the fun is finding just the right container to show off the gorgeous blooms. The uses to which fresh flowers can be put are limited only by imagination, and the collective imagination of Cape & Island residents is as endless as the sea. In the fall hydrangeas are harvested to make wreaths and floral arrangements that will last through the gray days of a New England winter, when touches of natural color in the home lift the spirits.

The popularity of the flower can be seen on the wide range of household products sporting hydrangea motifs including linens, pottery, Christmas ornaments, tableware, note cards, and art work. And when spring returns we plant hydrangeas where we can see them from inside the house; another way of bringing hydrangeas indoors.

We like to bring
hydrangeas inside
where we can see
them all the time.
A simple arrangement
of pink and blue
mopheads in a
cobalt blue bottle
adds vibrant color in a
South Yarmouth kitchen.

Having a range of colors in the garden outdoors contributes to a variety of colorful effects indoors.

Blue mopheads in a bowl decorated with blue hydrangeas over a plate decorated with yet more blue hydrangeas. It's easy to tell this homeowner loves hydrangeas.

Small hydrangea florets combined with blue Canterbury bells and pink Sweet William in a margarita glass. The shorter the stem of the cut hydrangea, the longer it will look fresh indoors. Flowers with stems this short can stay fresh for almost two weeks.

Lacecaps in early July in white metal container. This arrangement hangs at eye level making it easy to enjoy the beauty of these delicate-looking flowers.

A watering can decorated with hydrangeas in more ways than one.

Plastic pails are readily available all summer throughout the Cape & Islands and are great for informal arrangements.

A prize-winning entry in the Cape Cod Hydrangea Society's annual flower arranging contest. *Arrangement by Mary Cabral.*

Originally intended as a candle holder, this metal stand just needed shallow bowls set on top to hold the necessary water to keep these mopheads fresh.

Baskets make simple and lovely containers for hydrangeas. The soft green of this basket was just right to set off the deep blue of the flower.

Pink and blue mophead arrangement in a Nantucket basket.

Three wreaths just completed at a Cape Cod Hydrangea Society wreath making workshop. Each of these wreaths was a first-time effort by hydrangea society members.

Hydrangeas are harvested in the fall for flowers to be dried.
Some are used to make arrangements in vases while others are fashioned into popular wreaths.

A Dedham Pottery bowl decorated with the sand dollar motif holds a bounty of lacecaps.

Cape Clogs are decorated in many ways.
The hydrangea pattern is very popular.

A quilt featuring blue fabric with hydrangeas.
Quilt crafted by Ellen Whelan.

Tote bag with pink hydrangeas and quilt with blue hydrangeas.
Tote bag and quilt crafted by Ellen Whelan.

A Cape Cod Hydrangea Society member at the Society's display garden at Heritage Gardens in Sandwich.

Locally crafted white stoneware pottery in the popular hydrangea motif. The Chatham Pottery shop has devoted a whole wall to a wide variety of items featuring hydrangeas including dinnerware, mixing bowls, chowder bowls, mugs, platters, lamps, and wine caddies. *Pottery by Chatham Pottery owners Gill Wilson and Margaret Wilson-Grey.*

Two-tiered table hand-painted with a hydrangea theme. *Donna Laemmle, decorative artist.*

Bedding and area rug available at Snow's Home & Garden in Orleans. Many varieties of hydrangeas are sold in Snow's garden center.

The fabric of these curtains features hydrangeas in Nantucket baskets. Appropriately enough, the curtains hang in a Nantucket home.

Many items featuring hydrangeas can be found at The Mayflower Shop, a variety and gift store in Chatham center. These Chatham ornaments feature hydrangeas on sand dollars.

The hooked rug featuring hydrangeas in a Nantucket basket is much in demand at Claire Murray's many locations in the Cape & Islands.

The lobster on the towel at The Mayflower Shop seems to be reaching for the blue hydrangea on the neighboring towel.

Hydrangeas are popular motifs at the various outdoor art shows on Cape Cod. *Pictured art work by South Yarmouth artist, Diane Goers.*

Detail of a blue mophead hydrangea. *Art work by pastel artist Mary Anne Tessier of Yarmouth Port.*

A pair of ceramic tiles creating a scene with hydrangeas in the foreground and a couple in the distance walking along the sand. *"The Honeymooners" by Brewster artist Karen North Wells, the Underground Art Gallery.*

NOTABLE
HYDRANGEA DISPLAYS

While hydrangeas are dotted all over the Cape & Islands, there are some notable spots where you can see particularly outstanding displays. All of the gardens and garden centers noted below are open to the public.

An already substantial collection of hydrangeas is steadily growing at Heritage Gardens in Sandwich, where the Cape Cod Hydrangea Society has established its display garden. With its many varieties representing several species, the garden has already succeeded in its original goal, offering a garden that is both educational and beautiful. A climbing hydrangea graces the white arbor entrance to this not-to-be-missed garden.

Spohr Gardens in Falmouth is a lovely peaceful spot throughout the growing season. Hydrangea lovers should be sure to visit in spring when lush climbing hydrangeas scramble up many of the tall trees on the property.

Mal and Mary Kay Condon's Hydrangea Farm on Nantucket combines a display garden with a retail operation, an ideal place to see how the varieties you are considering for your own garden behave in a natural setting. This is one of the largest collections of hydrangeas in the eastern United States and is highly respected in the international hydrangea community.

The first hydrangeas in the Cape Cod Hydrangea Society's display garden at Heritage Gardens in Sandwich were planted in 2008 and the number of varieties has been growing ever since.

The climbing hydrangea scrambling up the garden arch represents one of the several species present in the display garden. Most of the varieties are in the *Hydrangea macrophylla* species (mopheads and lacecaps), but the visitor is also treated to many fine examples of *H. serrata, H. arborescens,* and *H. paniculata.*

Resort areas offer beautiful hydrangea displays, especially the Wequassett Resort on Pleasant Bay, Chatham Bars Inn, and the Chatham Wayside Inn.

The centers of many towns and villages are charming places to stroll while admiring the scenery. Hydrangeas are particularly lovely in Chatham, Harwich Port, Osterville, Oak Bluffs and Edgartown on Martha's Vineyard, and downtown Nantucket.

Areas close to the ocean are ideal for seeing countless beautiful displays of hydrangeas. The Hyannis Harbor area accents its artists' shanties with the Cape's signature blue hydrangeas and a long row of hydrangeas lines a walkway next to the water. The whole area around Hyannis Harbor is good for a walking tour. Don't miss Veterans Park next to the JFK Memorial on Ocean Avenue. Harbor areas in general are good locations for hydrangea spotting, especially Edgartown Harbor on Martha's Vineyard and Nantucket Harbor. The beach area of South Yarmouth is another good place to spot these lush blooms and not far from the beaches, the roads edging the Bass River are particularly lovely.

Cape & Island residents are lucky to have a good number of beautiful garden centers where the plants are healthy and the displays are inspirational. Because the plants are labeled, these are good locations for learning the names of hydrangea varieties to consider for one's own garden. Some of the best garden centers for hydrangeas are Country Garden in Hyannis, Hart Farm in Dennisport, Crocker Nurseries in Brewster, Agway of Cape Cod with locations in Dennis and Orleans, Mahoney's in Falmouth, the Green Spot Garden Center in South Yarmouth, Jardin Mahoney on Martha's Vineyard, and Mal and Mary Kay Condon's Hydrangea Farm on Nantucket.

Visitors to the Hydrangea Society's display garden in search of a particular color have the opportunity of seeing a wide range of colors displayed. 'Decatur Blue' is pictured here.

'Miss Belgium' at the Cape Cod Hydrangea Society's display garden in Sandwich.

'Bottstein' with both pink and blue flowers in early August, 2010.

Clear labels provide helpful information to visitors of the Hydrangea Society's display garden.

All of these hydrangea flower colors, shapes, and sizes (and more) can be found in the Cape Cod Hydrangea Society's display garden.

Country Garden in Hyannis offers beautiful displays of hydrangeas along with both practical and decorative items for the home gardener.

Exceptionally large hydrangea plants for sale at Country Garden in Hyannis.

Twenty-eight Atlantic, a popular restaurant at Wequassett Resort on Pleasant Bay, is located in this white building with the blue shutters and the magnificent hydrangea-filled garden out front.

Blue hydrangeas paired with yellow
daylilies at Wequassett Resort.

Hydrangeas and ornamental grass
grace a stone wall at Wequassett Resort.

Decorative planters come in many forms
at the Green Spot Garden Center.

A pink form of *Hydrangea arborescens* 'Annabelle' called Bella Anna™, part of the
Endless Summer® Collection, offered at the Green Spot Garden Center in South Yarmouth.

Hydrangeas form part of many decorative displays at the Green Spot Garden Center.

Many blue mopheads can be found throughout the grounds of the Chatham Bars Inn.

No matter where you look at the Chatham Bars Inn, you will see beautiful waves of healthy hydrangeas. Masses of them are located near the doors entering from the parking lot.

A large blue mophead hydrangea shrub flourishes in the bracing sea air at the Chatham Bars Inn.

Cape Cod, home of the Cape Cod Baseball League, is a logical place to offer baseball-themed stepping stones. The pictured stepping stone was spotted at the Green Spot Garden Center.

Wonderful hydrangeas can be found all over the island of Martha's Vineyard. This gingerbread house in Oak Bluffs has a fine display of lacecaps out front.

A classic combination: blue hydrangeas and
a white house. Edgartown, Martha's Vineyard.

An Edgartown front door on Martha's Vineyard.

Hydrangea macrophylla 'Ayesha'
in a Nantucket window box.

A flag waves in the ocean breeze
over these Nantucket hydrangeas.

Nantucket is well known for its beautiful hydrangeas. The straight lines of this house with
its weathered shingles are softened by the round hydrangea flowers on the curved fences.

The flower beds at the Condon's Hydrangea Farm on Nantucket sport varieties of many colors. These lovely white flowers are 'Queen of Pearls'.

Stroll along the wharf areas at Nantucket Harbor to see many colorful healthy hydrangeas.

Hydrangeas gracing flower beds outside Mal and Mary Kay Condon's home on Nantucket.

Outside the office at the Condon's Hydrangea Farm.

Landscaping ideas using hydrangeas are easy to find at the Hydrangea Farm on Nantucket.

Lush flower beds surround the farmhouse at the Condon's Hydrangea Farm.

With over two hundred different varieties, it's hard to choose a favorite at the Hydrangea Farm. Pictured here is the unusual 'Hopcorn'.

An artist's inspiration at the Condon's Hydrangea Farm.

When members of the Cape Cod Hydrangea Society made a field trip to the Hydrangea Farm on Nantucket, most of them fell in love with this variety called 'Brestenberg'.

HYDRANGEA MEMORIES

The sight of a blue hydrangea can trigger a cascade of Cape & Island memories. So strong is our association of this cheerful blue flower with this particular part of the world that the mind is suddenly flooded with images of sand and sea and sky and blissful relaxed days away from the routine of everyday life. We remember bike rides and sailing and swimming and golf. We feel the sand under our feet and the sun on our shoulders. We smell salty air and fried clams and fresh blueberry pies cooling on kitchen counters. We hear the cries of the seagulls, the squeak of the screen door, and the crash of the big surf on the seashore. We are whisked back to our childhood when we walked down lanes lined with hydrangeas spilling over split rail fences. We remember the simple pleasure of choosing just the right ice cream flavor at the end of a fun day at the beach. Beach balls bounce through our memories along with sand castles and riding the waves and burying our feet in the sand.

We remember the magic of taking a ferry to an island and the beauty of that island when we arrived. We remember the salt spray and mist and fog and the sound of foghorns. Fog is so common on Nantucket that it is nicknamed "The Grey Lady" and, lucky for us, hydrangeas look particularly lovely in the fog and mist. Beautiful colors in soft focus – how can you go wrong? We remember pouring off ferries into the embrace of charming seaside villages where hydrangeas seem to be part of every delightful scene.

Vivid blue hydrangeas are to gardens on the Cape & Islands as lighthouses are to the shoreline; they look just right. They complete the picture. They satisfy something deep in our spirit. It is impossible to imagine Cape Cod & the Islands without hydrangeas. They are essential. They are quintessential. They perfectly represent what we all long for; endless summer.

Colorful mophead hydrangeas in front of a Harwich Port cottage.

Perhaps this bicycle parked in a bike stand at Hyannis Harbor belongs to a summer employee of a nearby restaurant.

Summer memories for countless Cape Cod visitors include walking past weathered cottages with their almost obligatory hydrangeas to get from the beach to the seafood restaurant across the street.

Cape Cod, ice cream, and hydrangeas. How can you go wrong? The Cape Cod Creamery, South Yarmouth.

Hydrangea lovers enjoy attending Sundae School.

Hydrangeas and sailors both love the ocean.

Beautiful hydrangeas make relaxing
in a hammock even more pleasurable.

Any home with blue hydrangeas in the yard can just
add an American flag to be well decked out for the
Fourth of July.

Waterfront dining is even better
when hydrangeas grace the scene.

A laid-back dog is keeping an eye on the action at the Satucket Farm Stand in Brewster.

Visual reminders of the sea. Blue hydrangeas at Hyannis Harbor.

Visitors happily dedicate themselves to relaxing on Cape Cod & the Islands. This chair outside the Chatham Wayside Inn is a great spot from which to watch the passing scene on Main Street.

The closer to the ocean the better, as far as hydrangeas are concerned.

An inviting porch on a summer day with salty air and the cool blue of hydrangeas.

A ride on a swing is even better with beautiful hydrangeas in the picture.

Visual delights abound throughout the Cape & Islands. Where else will you get unexpected glimpses of mermaids on weathervanes? The hydrangeas caught the photographer's eye first. The mermaid was a bonus. Spotted in Edgartown, looking toward the harbor.

A lush row of hydrangeas edges the lawn at Wychmere Harbor, a frequent site of outdoor weddings.

A study in blue at the Surfcomber motel
on Nantucket Sound in South Yarmouth.

This blue hydrangea seems to draw
us in to this cool retreat on Nantucket.

All roads, and driveways, on Cape Cod and the Islands seem to lead to hydrangeas.

The rich vibrant colors of hydrangeas in this lovely part of the world bestow the gift of natural beauty.

Lovely lacecaps outside the Blue Water Bakery Café on South Wharf on Nantucket.

Summer memories of Cape Cod and the Islands include mystical mornings in the fog and mist.

Mophead hydrangeas outside the Beach House Grill at Chatham Bars Inn.

A relaxing spot for outdoor enjoyment: comfortable wicker chairs on a porch surrounded by hydrangeas.

With hydrangeas flourishing in this climate, it's easy to see why homeowners add many hydrangeas to their gardens.

A South Yarmouth home with a classic Cape Cod looks complete with blue hydrangeas.

Lacecaps and mopheads outside a Cape Cod home.

An award-winning arrangement on Nantucket.

It looks as if the address should be Hydrangea House, Cape Cod, Massachusetts.

A favorite chair, a favorite porch, a favorite Cape & Islands location, and a favorite blue flower. This is the life!

INDEX